a Gift for

_____

From

_____

How Great Our *Joy*

BROADMAN & HOLMAN PUBLISHERS • NASHVILLE, TENNESSEE

Contents

7: Part One

Don't Forget the Joy!

33: Part Two

Majesty in a Manger

61: Part Three

The Birth of Christ, the Death of Sin

89: Part Four

Bow and Worship Him

105: Part Five

Immanuel Will Be with You

Introduction

It's Thanksgiving evening. About fifteen Ortlund family members are crowded into daughter Margie and John's living room. We're all more stuffed than the turkey was earlier, and everybody's mellowed out.

Then suddenly Margie cries, "Is Thanksgiving over yet?"

We all shout, "Yes!" (We do it every year; it's a family tradition thing.)

And Margie bellows, *"Merry Christmas!"* while simultaneously starting Christmas music on the stereo. With that, for the Ortlunds, the Christmas season has begun for another year.

And we say to you as you pick up this book: This is a new time for you, too.

You've never lived this Christmas before.

You're at a new place in your life. So much has happened to you since last Christmas!

Sure, the truths of Christmas aren't new; they were established before the foundation of the world. The story of Christmas itself is two thousand years old.

But for you and us, this Christmas season is brand new.

So be blessed by this book. Be deepened. Keep praising.

Have a merry, most joyful Christmas!

Part One

Don't Forget the Joy!

In the same region, shepherds were living out in the fields and keeping watch at night over their flock. Then an angel of the Lord stood before them . . . and they were terrified. But the angel said to them, "Do not be afraid, for you see, I announce to you good news of great joy that will be for all the people: because today in the city of David was born for you a Savior, who is Christ the Lord." Luke 2:8–11

What will occupy you most this Christmas season:

burdens or Joys?

The shepherds that first Christmas night were probably burdened . . . with all the usual culprits: straying lambs, wool ticks, cut hooves, nighttime cold.

Then suddenly they were exposed to angels, international news, and glory — *brilliant, radiant,* *Shekinah Glory!*

They could never be the same again.

The shepherds returned *"glorifying and praising God for all they had seen and heard"* (Luke 2:20). Sure, they returned to wool ticks and cut hooves, but forever after they would see all their annoyances through new eyes.

Christian, are you burdened with the "usual"?

You, too, have been exposed to all the splendor, all the joy, all the majesty of God's eternal plans, set in motion by the birth of Jesus.

Then don't be absorbed by the burdens! Do your daily work this Christmas *glorifying and praising God for all you have seen and heard.*

The shepherds returned, glorifying and praising God for all they had seen and heard.

Luke 2:20

Oh, ring Noel,
Each loud Christmas bell;
God's good news is great news
all over the earth!
And Christians—all sing it
As bells ring and ring it;
Applaud it and laud it,
this wonderful birth!
Yes, ring it out, fling it out,
chiming and clanging:
On this joyous morn
Our Redeemer is born!

Can the world celebrate something it doesn't understand?

People of this world string their Christmas lights, not fully realizing that their decorations are saying to believers, *"Arise, shine, for your light has come, and the glory of the LORD rises upon you"* (Isaiah 60:1, NIV). They punch in their CDs that sing, "Oh, come let us adore Him, Christ the Lord!"

Matthew 13:13,16 says, *"Looking they do not see, and hearing they do not listen or understand. . . . But your eyes are blessed because they do see, and your ears because they do hear!"*

So this holiday season, don't be a Scrooge. Don't grumble over the commercialization of Christmas. *Blessed are your eyes and ears that can comprehend what all this beauty really means.*

Do the sights and sounds of Christmas draw you a little higher?

Drink in. Cherish it. Rejoice! And pray that some who have lived in the dark all year long will find the Light of the world in the lights of Christmas.

At this new Christmas season, worship Him. Between your ears, within your heart, where no one sees but God alone—worship Him!

Often confess your sins to Him. Often think on His characteristics. From moment to moment, as much as you're able, keep a running conversation going with your Father.

He will love it.

Worship Him

As you move through the Christmas lights
and beauty, worship Him.

As you write your cards, worship Him.

As you trim your tree, worship Him.

As you spend, be spent.

As you serve others, serve Him.

Let your heart keep welling up with
"glory to God in the highest!"

What joy the Christ of Christmas brings,

And life and peace and all good things!

Be full, our friends,

Filled to the brim;

Be full of joy,

Be full of Him.

Could you use a fill-up in your joy compartment?

When Elizabeth, the mother of John the Baptist, *"was filled with the Holy Spirit . . . she exclaimed with a loud cry: 'Blessed are you among women, and blessed is your offspring!'"* (Luke 1:41,42).

When her husband Zechariah *"was filled with the Holy Spirit,"* he prophesied, *"Blessed is the Lord"* (Luke 1:67,68).

Even their baby, John, was *"filled with the Holy Spirit while still in his mother's womb"* (Luke 1:15). And when he grew up, he went everywhere preaching as *"a voice of one crying out in the wilderness"* (Luke 3:4).

Be filled with the *Holy Spirit!*

Mary, after the most amazing of all fillings of the Holy Spirit, exclaimed, *"My soul proclaims the greatness of the Lord. . . . Holy is His name"* (Luke 1:46,49).

Pick up the Christmas tradition started by these early ones. They were all filled with the Holy Spirit, and they opened their mouths in joyful praise.

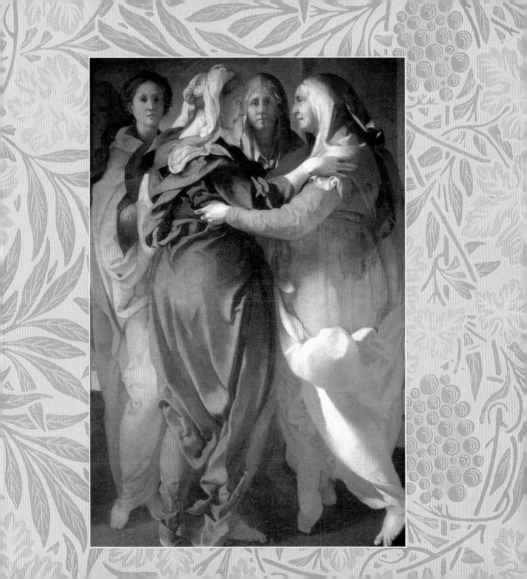

Family Reflections

We're gathered around the table after Christmas dinner, and I,
the matriarch of the Ortlund tribe, ask the family a question:

"Do you know what the four stages of life are? Stage one: you believe in Santa Claus. Stage two: you don't believe in Santa Claus. Stage three: you are Santa Claus. Stage four: you look like Santa Claus!"

Everybody guffaws.

The pushed-back, peaceful moments after Christmas dinner are a time when we always contribute our silly holiday humor; it's another family tradition.

Firstborn Sherry pipes up (I'll identify each one: husband Walt Harrah writes, arranges, sings, and produces Christian music): "Have you heard this one? A Russian named Rudolph looks out the window to check the weather. 'It's raining,' he says. But his wife replies, 'No, I think that's snow.' 'It's rain,' says Rudolph. 'Snow,' says his wife. Finally, Rudolph ends the debate once and for all: "Rudolph the Red knows rain, dear.' "

Loud Ortlund groans.

We also pass out silly Christmas greeting cards; everybody's brought a few. (We bring silly cards to our family birthday parties, too.) Second-born Margie (husband John McClure is a pastor in Newport Beach) has deviated from tradition.

She's brought a Hanukkah card: Moses is on the mountain, kneeling in front of the two completed tablets of the law. He looks up and says, "Lord, we've got a little extra space here at the bottom. Want to put something about brushing after meals?"

Ray, Jr. (a pastor in Augusta, Georgia) throws his head back and laughs so hard he cackles, and pretty soon everybody's laughing at Ray laughing.

Fourth child Nels (a policeman in Monrovia, California) has forgotten his cards, but off-the-cuff he contributes something else: "Did you hear about the traveling salesman who saw a three-legged chicken run across the road in front of him and into a farmyard? Well, he couldn't resist. He stopped his car and said to the farmer, 'Hey, do you know you've got a chicken with three legs?' 'Yeah, all our chickens got three legs,' said the farmer. 'We done bred 'em that way.' 'Why?' asked the salesman. 'Because folks like extra drumsticks.' The salesman was amazed. 'How do they taste?' he asked. 'We don't know,' said the farmer. 'We ain't never been able to catch one!'"

"That has nothing to do with Christmas!" we all howl. Then we pelt him with wadded-up, used Christmas wrappings until he's pretty much buried.

Enjoy!

Enjoy the Christ of Christmas!

Enjoy the ones you love!

For "every good and perfect gift

Cometh from above."

Have you heard what the angels are saying?

Several times in history, God has poked a hole through the sky and let His divine joy shine down on us.

When Solomon first dedicated God's temple, fire came down from heaven and consumed the burnt offerings, and the priests couldn't go inside the temple because the glory of the Lord had filled it like a cloud.

And at the first Christmas, when God's Son arrived, He sent a vast array of angels singing thrilling songs, as well as a very special, shining, mystical star. God pulled out the stops!

The words of the angels' song recorded in Luke 2:14 were full of joy: *"Glory to God in the highest heaven, and peace on earth to people He favors!"*

Have you forgotten where you left your joy?

Jesus' first coming to earth can still result in glory to God and peace on earth. That's revival, renewal!

The two of us have seen it happen over and over, as God's people in missions groups or churches—dry, tired, bugged at each other—have experienced His Spirit's cleansing and refreshing. Invariably, their faces shine with a renewed sense of glory to God, and their hearts swell with a desire for restored peace among men.

And then—oh, how they sing!

Could you use a little of that right now?

Tell Him today. *And don't forget the joy!*

Joy!

Try to catch the scope of their song:

*Those in the highest places in heaven
eternally enjoy His glory.*

*Those on earth—through all ages
of human history—can enjoy His peace.*

*All heaven and earth are deeply affected
with joy by the birth of Christ.*

For you and us another year has fled,

And varied are the ways that God has led.

But if the year brought stress to you,

Or loss,

Christ came to bear them all

Upon His cross.

So Christmas joy is deep

And good

And strong.

Look up, our friend,

And sing a Christmas song!

Part Two

Majesty in a Manger

This will be a sign for you: you will find a baby

wrapped snugly in cloth and lying in a manger.

Luke 2:12

Consider how

His star shone down,

Revealing cradle,

Cross,

And crown.

"*Lift up your heads, O you gates!*
Be lifted up, you ancient doors,
That the King of glory may come in!"

(Psalm 24:7, NIV)

That Christmas day the King came in!
He pushed our hearts' doors open wide
(So long closed up by pain and sin)
and strode inside.

"*Who is this King of glory?*"
"*The* LORD *strong and mighty,*
The LORD *mighty in battle*"

(Psalm 24:8, NIV)

But, oh, You came so meek and soft,

Surprising us with baby form

And stars and song and cattle loft and hay so warm.

Our King of Glory!

How can we express

The wonder of your power and graciousness?

What made Christ's coming unlike any other, unlike any since?

A number of "comings" in secular history had awesome effects on their day. Napoleon, for example, in 1815. The year before, he had been banished from France to Elba, and it looked as if that were the end of Napoleon.

But even while separated from his homeland, he had been keeping up with events. In March 1815—barely a year after his exile—having gotten word about how weak and unpopular his successor (Louis XVIII) was, and knowing that the common people of France still wished for him, Napoleon went back to France.

The emperor heard that Napoleon had returned, and he sent a whole army out to capture him. As the army advanced toward him, Napoleon got out of his carriage and started walking toward the oncoming troops. He was alone; he was defenseless. He just walked right toward them! And when he got close enough, he opened his coat, so that if they chose to fire they could aim right at his heart. And he said quietly, "Frenchmen, it's your emperor."

The soldiers went wild. They kissed his hands. They fell at his feet. They picked him up and carried him on their shoulders, and they roared at the top of their lungs, "Long live the Emperor! Long live the Emperor!"

Two thousand years ago, a much greater King came among the people—and His coming was even quieter, humbler, and more vulnerable.

Here's how Luke 2 describes it:

"While [Joseph and Mary] were [in Bethlehem], it happened that the days were completed for her to give birth. Then she gave birth to her firstborn Son, and she wrapped Him snugly in cloth and laid Him in a manger—because there was no room for them at the inn."

Hebrews 10:5-7 describes it in a larger perspective:

"As He was coming into the world, He said: . . . You prepared a body for Me. . . . I have come . . . to do your will, O God!"

Titus 3:4–5 steps back still farther, picturing Christ's coming in maybe the most awesome way of all: *"When the goodness and love for man appeared from God our Savior, He saved us."*

Like Napoleon, but far vaster in scope, Christ arrived, saying, "My children, it's your Savior."

What a coming!

Come...

Christ has come to you.

Now you come to Him.

Come humbly, as the shepherds did.

Come bringing gifts, as the wise men did.

But come!

O come, dear friend,

to the Christmas Child,

To a Baby soft with His

Head laid down.

Oh, kneel at His crib.

When you lift your eyes,

A Man from a cross

Will have cleft the skies,

And His head will shine

With a dazzling crown!

What if Christ had not come that first Christmas?

For one thing, the world would still be caught in the death-hold of slavery. When Christ was born, three out of every five humans were slaves. The clanking of chains could be heard everywhere. Roman law said that if you killed someone's ox, you paid for it with your own life. But if you killed a slave — no problem!

But, oh, the coming of Christ rang the deathknell of slavery! Even today as His principles are taught, slavery shrinks and disappears. One day it will be gone altogether.

If Christ had not come, women everywhere would still be used and abused. When Christ was born, women were considered inconsequential and a burden, good only for their ability to produce children and for the contributions of their toil and work.

But Jesus was a champion of women! They were some of His dearest friends. Women were the last to be with Him at His death and the first to see Him at His resurrection. And through the centuries since, when His principles are upheld, women acquire a place of dignity, honor, and worth in society.

Jesus touched lepers, loved the poor, held children on His lap, comforted widows, and healed the sick. He told us what things are important—not "things" but people. *"What is a man benefited,"* He challenged us, *"if he gains the whole world, yet loses or forfeits himself?"* (Luke 9:25).

And ever since, the truest test of any civilization's worth isn't the skyscrapers it builds or the accumulation of wealth or technology it produces, but rather the way it cares for its weakest, poorest, and most vulnerable. Stocks won't last; crops won't last; computer chips won't last; but the least human beings will last for all eternity.

In Matthew 13, He called us a treasure.

In Luke 15, He compared us to sheep and promised that the Good Shepherd would go through anything to find even one of us that gets lost!

*If Christ hadn't come, we'd have never understood
the preciousness of one soul —
the preciousness of you, our friend —
in the sight of God.*

When Christ was born on Christmas morn,

A dream was born of infinite care

That you and I would find a cross —

And meet Him there.

When Christ was born on Christmas morn,

A dream was born of glorious worth,

That wolves and lambs would dwell in peace

And latter rains make crops increase

On all the earth.

When Christ was born on Christmas morn,

A dream was born—God's own great scheme

That sin and death would soon be past

And kingdom peace emerge at last.

Oh, friend, be glad!

Look up! Hold fast

the
Christmas
Dream!

When Jesus was born…

The present heavens knew their end was near—
When the stars would drop like shriveled figs,
The sky be rolled up like an old parchment scroll,
And the sun and moon be replaced by
The Lord, our Light.

When Jesus was born…

The present earth knew it was terminal.
A new one would emerge
Where wolves, lambs, lions, and oxen all browse together,
And snakes eat dust, and dust only,
And nothing will hurt or destroy
On all God's holy mountain.

When Jesus was born...

Weakness was condemned to death,

And so was death itself, and waste and sickness

And frustration and alarm and fatigue,

And insensitivity, complacency, mediocrity, deceit,

Greed, laziness, egocentricity, and all the rest.

When Jesus was born...

So was hope!

The way was paved for the Kingdom, when all our

Inventing, organizing, creating, producing, and

Tweaking will be uninhibited!

And we'll plant with expectation and reap with joy!

And a thousand, thousand dreams will come true.

Think about what Jesus started,
And have a Merry Christmas!

What do you name a baby who was sent to save the world?

Hear the angel's message from God the Father to Joseph:

"[Mary] will give birth to a son, and you are to name Him Jesus, because He will save His people from their sins" (Matthew 1:21).

Yet the Bible also gives many other names of Jesus to explain the wonder and majesty of His person. He is Light, Life, the Word, the Alpha and Omega, the Head of the body, the Ancient of Days, and plenty more. But His most loved name, His Christmas name—Jesus—is the key to understanding all the others.

Interestingly, none of His disciples are recorded as calling Him "Jesus" to His face. They called Him "Lord," "Master," "Teacher," "Rabbi," but they never addressed Him as "Jesus."

Maybe they felt His name was too sacred to use in His presence. Only later would they write of Him as "Jesus" or "Lord Jesus" or "the Lord Jesus Christ."

They understood that there was power in that name.

Peter said to a lame man, *"I have neither silver nor gold, but what I have, I give to you: In the name of Jesus Christ the Nazarene, get up and walk!... So [the man] jumped up, stood, and started to walk"* (Acts 3:6,8).

No wonder Paul lifted up that name and wrote, "At the name of Jesus every knee should bow—of those who are in heaven and on earth and under the earth" (Philippians 2:10).

Our friend—love and honor His Christmas name! Speak it with care. Believe what it means, and call His name *"Jesus, because He will save His people from their sins."*

The word "He" in that sentence is placed in the emphatic position, meaning that He and He alone would save His people.

"There is salvation in no one else, for there is no other name under heaven given to people by which we must be saved" (Acts 4:12).

He and He alone, all by Himself, would purge away our sins. And none of His saving work would be left undone! He began the saving; He continued it; and He finished it. Jesus is the perfect, complete Savior.

"He will save his people from their sins."

If what we needed most was a philosopher or a political leader, God would have sent His Son to be that. But what we needed most was a Savior from our sins. And—praise God— we have one.

His
name
is *Jesus*

Praise the Lord from the heavens!

Praise Him, all you heavenly hosts,

Sun and moon and shining stars!

Praise the Lord from the earth!

Great sea creatures, ocean depths,

Mountains and all hills,

Trees, wild animals, cattle!

Praise Him, magi and shepherds—all flesh!

Praise Him in holy Christmas joy!

The Center of the Center

Is a tiny Boy,

And all the universe

His creche.

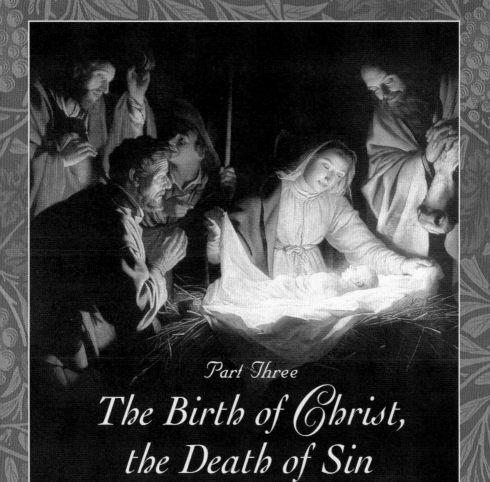

Part Three

The Birth of Christ, the Death of Sin

"*Indeed, this child is destined to cause the fall and rise of many in Israel, and to be a sign that will be opposed— and a sword will pierce your own soul—that the thoughts of many hearts may be revealed.*"

Luke 2:34–35

Christmas was planned before winters or springs,
    Before lions had paws, before sparrows had wings.
But then came Creation—and rabbits and fish
    And donkeys and people; they all wished one wish:
"We wish that we weren't so afraid of each other,
    That folks wouldn't quarrel or brother hate brother!"
Then finally came Christmas:
    The Word was made flesh,
And dear Baby Jesus was laid in a creche.

Sleep, Baby, sleep: The Kingdom will come.
    Lions, rabbits—be of good cheer!
Sing, angels, sing—no longer be dumb;
    Tell the great story:
            The Savior is here!

Family Reflections

It was the week before Christmas in Pasadena, California. Ray was pastor of the Lake Avenue Congregational Church there, so he was a little bit known. Or did this phone call come from somebody's looking in the Yellow Pages?

Anyway, we got a call from (of all places) Los Angeles' Juvenile Hall, part of the city's correctional facilities. *Would our family come give them a program on Christmas morning?*

We quickly commenced a group powwow. "It could be our family's Christmas present to Jesus," Ray said. So we agreed. While I played the piano, Ray and the children would sing a "special Christmas number." Then each of us would share something from a Christmas Scripture verse: I, Sherry, Margie, Ray, Jr., Bud—they were all high schoolers. Then Dad would preach.

Early Christmas morning (no presents yet, not even stocking gifts) we dressed and drove to downtown L.A. and parked in the cold, gray parking lot of this giant, cold, gray building. A series of cold, gray doors opened for us and clanged shut behind us, and we were ushered into a huge, cold, gray assembly hall.

Soon a few hundred boys filed in, from little ones through the teen years, shepherded by plenty of guards. They noisily piled into their chairs, heads down, looking so defeated, so despondent! Christmas morning—and they were so far from home . . . (if they had homes)! We "did our thing" with aching hearts, and then the boys filed out.

In a few minutes a few hundred girls came spilling in, again accompanied by those ever-present guards, and they, too, noisily piled into the chairs with their heads down and eyes averted. I groaned a wordless prayer: "Oh, Lord—"

Before our turn came, a girls' choir filed across the front and began to sway and sing "Sweet Little Jesus Boy," cuddled in tender, soft rock. Christmas morning! It was too much. A girl in the crowd began to cry—out loud! Another girl began to cry. Another began to wail— girls in jail on Christmas, realizing how badly they'd blown it because "they didn't know who [He] was." Soon they were all wailing, and the wailing grew louder into an anguished roar, a sustained scream! The large hall nearly burst with the deafening reverberations.

It was over almost before it started. The guards led the girls out. The choir number never got finished. We didn't sing; we didn't speak; Ray didn't even preach. The guards escorted us out of the cold, gray assembly hall, through the same series of cold, gray doors clanging shut behind us, and out into the cold, gray parking lot. We drove home.

Oh, the pain of sin!

Long time before, old Simeon had prophesied to Mary: *"Indeed, this child is destined to cause the fall and rise of many . . . and to be a sign that will be opposed—and a sword will pierce your own soul— that the thoughts of many hearts may be revealed"* (Luke 2:34,35).

Christmas ushered in the eventual falling of many people: *Nero. Hitler. Stalin.*

Us. You.

The teenagers in Juvenile Hall.

Everybody.

We all have fallen.

"There is no one righteous, not even one. . . . All have turned away, together they have become useless" (Romans 3:10,12). Even *"all our righteous acts are like filthy rags"* (Isaiah 64:6, NIV)

And this Christmas Child Himself, when He was grown, said, *"The Father, in fact, judges no one but has given all judgment to the Son. . . . He has granted Him the right to pass judgment, because He is the Son of Man"* (John 5:22,27).

So this Child was destined to be the Great and Final Judge, when *"the thoughts of many hearts [will] be revealed."*

BUT—it would be too heart-stopping, too anguishing, too terrible to contemplate if this Child had not also been destined to cause the rising of many!

"Who is this?" asked Isaiah many centuries before Jesus was born, *"robed in splendor, striding forward in the greatness of his strength?"*

And the Eternal Christ Himself answered, *"It is I, speaking in righteousness, mighty to save."*

"Why are your garments red," the prophet asked, *"like those of one treading the winepress?"*

"I have trodden the winepress alone. . . . There was no one to help . . . so my own arm worked salvation for me" (Isaiah 63:1-3,5, NIV).

So, *"When the completion of the time came, God sent His Son, born of a woman"* (Galatians 4:4).

And the Christmas angel told Joseph, *"You are to name Him Jesus, because He will save His people from their sins"* (Matthew 1:21).

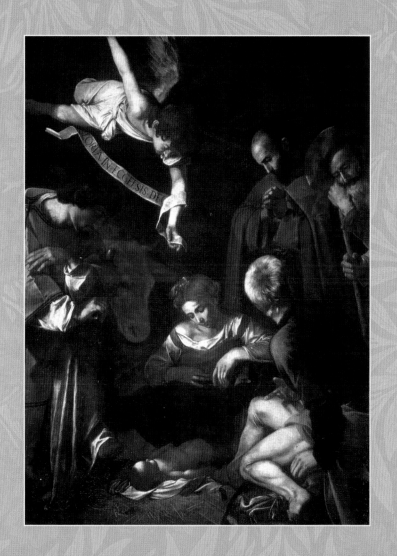

What if we told you the most expensive gift was for you?

There's a deep, rumbling, groaning echo of sadness when we think about what it meant for God the Father to send His Son from heaven. John 3:17 gives us a hint of this: *"For God did not send His Son into the world that He might judge the world, but that the world might be saved through Him."*

The original Greek word "send" could be translated, "He did not *send off* his Son into the world." When Christ was "sent off," it meant separation between the Father and His beloved Son. He "sent Him off" to save the world, the verse says, and yet the Father knew that the world would thank Him for His act of loving mercy by buffeting the Son, abusing Him, murdering Him. Can you imagine how the Father had to feel, when He "sent off" His lovely Son?

One of the most loved of all Scriptures is John 3:16: *"For God loved the world in this way: He gave His only Son, so that everyone who believes in Him will not perish but have eternal life."*

God emptied heaven! None was so precious to Him as His only Son, yet He gave Him. But, friends, the sacrifice began long before the cross, and it was a sacrifice full of emotion. There was joy in knowing the ultimate victory of the resurrection, yet there was also deep grief.

Don't take lightly the cost of Christmas to God the Father. Love was behind it all. Love was the reason—the only reason—that Almighty God was willing to pay such a dreadful price.

And don't take lightly the cost of Christmas to Christ the Son. John writes, *"In the beginning was the Word; and the Word was with God, and the Word was God"* (John 1:1). The original Greek word "with" could be translated "the Son was facing the Father." It implies a deep intimacy between Them in all the pasts of eternity. Before there was our universe, there was the Holy Trinity.

Jesus, just before His cross, commented on the glory of this fellowship: *"Now, Father, glorify Me in your presence with that glory I had with You before the world existed"* (John 17:5). A splendor—a radiance—had existed in the Father-Son relationship which, at the first Christmas, necessarily had to change. For thirty-three years, They would both miss it.

Second Corinthians 8:9 gives us this tender explanation of the cost of Christmas to Jesus: *"For you know the grace of our Lord Jesus Christ: although He was rich, for your sake He became poor, so that by His poverty you might become rich."*

"By His poverty!" How poor did Christ become?

First, our glorious Second Person of the Godhead became a baby—a vulnerable, human baby—dependent on Joseph and Mary to feed and clothe and protect Him. A baby has nothing.

Second, He grew up as a "nobody," a man *"of no reputation"* (Philippians 2:7, KJV). Throughout eternity past, all heaven had adored and worshiped Him. Suddenly on earth, His true identity was unknown; His claims were discounted. People even called Him a blasphemer or (worse) a demoniac!

Third, He was nailed to a cross, bearing all the sin of the world, and rejected completely by His own, beloved, eternal Abba.

Oh, the cost of Christmas to Christ the Son! Don't take it lightly!

And yet He endured it all *"for the joy that lay before Him"* (Hebrews 12:2). The joy of making you rich! The joy of forgiving your sins and reconciling you to the Father! The joy of providing you with access to the riches of God's glory through prayer! The joy of giving you a loving family of God! The joy of opening for you the doors of heaven and lavishing on you His love and care until you get there!

Praise God for Christmas! Praise God that He was willing to pay the cost—every last penny of it! Praise God for His incredible grace! It truly is, for us . . .

Great Riches At Christ's Expense!

For you know the grace of our Lord Jesus Christ: although He was rich, for your sake He became poor, so that by His poverty you might become rich.

2 Corinthians 8:9

The Spirit brooded,

Brooded over dawn's creation

Till life and breath invaded everything,

And cows began to calve, and birds to sing,

And Adam grew to be a mighty nation.

The Spirit brooded,

Brooded over humble Mary —

That little maid, the overshadowed one —

Till He who formed in her was God's great Son,

The eternal Christ,

And she, His sanctuary.

Please, Spirit, brood—

Oh, brood upon Your waiting people!

Look down on groaning earth and groaning men;

Revive us, shake us, wake us!

Brood again—till glory lights our land,

And every tree's a steeple!

Got anything under that tree for the pain in our heels?

Listen carefully to the story of Christmas, and you can hear in the background the quiet, sinister hiss of a serpent. In fact, a writhing snake tail whipped about the heels of ancient history, trying its best to topple the whole event.

"S-s-s-s," the serpent breathed to Eve long before the first Christmas morn, and she ate the forbidden fruit and gave some to her husband, too.

But—(this is amazing!)—along with His punishments for Adam and Eve's sin, God simultaneously showed His incredible mercy and tender love, and He gave them (and us) this incredible hope: The woman's offspring, Jesus Christ, would ultimately crush Satan's head with a finishing blow, though the serpent would continue to strike the offspring's heel — painful punches, but not mortal blows (Genesis 3:15).

Through succeeding centuries the serpent kept striking and striking, trying to cut off the Christ to come.

"S-s-s-s," he breathed to Egypt's Pharaoh, who tried in Exodus 1 to murder all Jewish boy babies. He failed.

"S-s-s-s," he breathed again to Persia's King Xerxes, who tried in Esther 3 to wipe out all the Jews. The plot was aborted.

"S-s-s-s," he breathed in a last-ditch effort to Judea's King Herod, who tried in Matthew 2 to kill all Hebrew boy babies age two and under. But Joseph was warned in a dream and fled the country with his wife, Mary, and the universe's tiny new treasure, Jesus.

Ultimately, God's promise will prove true,

and Christ Jesus will triumph!

But for now, that first damaging blow inflicted on Adam and Eve has temporarily brought misery to all their descendants. *"Just as sin entered the world through one man, and death through sin, in this way death spread to all men, because all sinned"* (Romans 5:12).

Now, in a larger sense, the first couple's "offspring" includes all of us human beings. And ever since those two fell to the serpent's temptation, we've all known pain in our heels! *"The ancient serpent, who is called the Devil and Satan, the one who deceives the whole world"* (Revelation 12:9) continues to strike with his venomous bite, and we're all made miserable from it.

The two of us—Anne and Ray—are a microcosm of that. We are the "Adam and Eve" of our particular Ortlund tribe.

We were both raised carefully in godly homes where (to us) smoking a cigarette or going to a movie were unthinkable sins! But, still, the seeds of disobedience were alive and well within us both. In our early marriage, when some conflict would arise—

"S-s-s-s" could be heard hissing from somewhere in the house, and I, Anne, would get strong willed and accusatory, and I'd enflame the situation.

"S-s-s-s" would keep on breathing in the background, and I, Ray, would get defensive and hostile.

For within the two of us is every potential for every kind of evil. God (for His own mysterious reasons) has sheltered us from dysfunctional families and drugs and murders and prison sentences, but it's no credit to the two of us! Left to ourselves, we are easy prey for that "ancient serpent" that keeps writhing and striking our heels.

Even our offspring (now up to three generations, so far) deal with their own set of struggles against strong wills and defensiveness and every kind of misery! We bow our heads and know that the seeds of those things were within us, and when we bore children, we reproduced not only ourselves but also our sins.

Children, we are sorry! We repent a thousand times!

We apologize to you! Please forgive us.

But that first Christmas shouted loud and clear that the serpent was losing and that Christ would win. The reason Satan makes us all miserable, sometimes, is simply because he's a poor loser: *"For the Devil has come down to you with great fury, because he knows he has a short time"* (Revelation 12:12).

The Ortlund family celebrations—our gifts and songs and laughter and prayers—are not glib and superficial. We are tenderly aware of one another's depressions, battles, struggles, and miseries. We hold one another's hands and hug a lot, to get each other through.

Our heels hurt.

But those hurts, though painful, aren't ultimate. Christ, the victorious Christmas Child, is the ultimate One!

Soon He will crush Satan's head. And He shall save His people—including us—from our sins!

Cool!—as our kids would say.

Ye-ow!—as our grandkids would say.

Our great grandkids don't say nuthin'—yet.

But they will.

Oh, the beauty of the Christmas season,

Celebration of the Baby's birth!

Jesus Christ our Savior is the reason

Lights are glowing now around the earth.

May the light invade as well within,

Chasing out the dark of personal sin!

Holy,

Holy,

Holy is the Boy.

Holy be your peace; and pure, your joy.

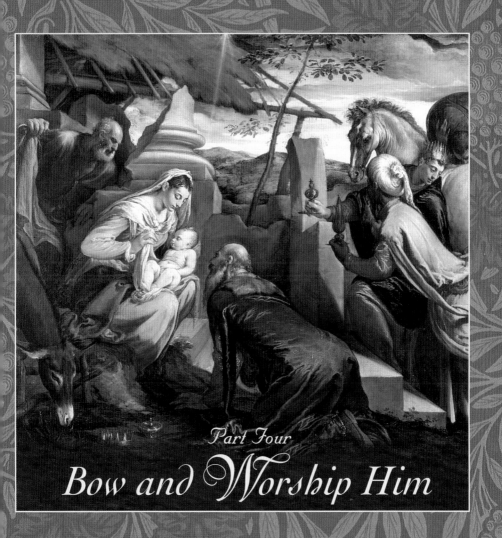

Part Four

Bow and Worship Him

They saw the child with Mary His mother,

and falling to their knees, they worshiped Him.

Matthew 2:11

Dear Christmas Jesus,
Tucked in your bed,
Cows at Your feet, Lord,
Lambs at Your head:
Say, did they know You,
There in the shed?

Whether they knew You
There in the stall,
Heaven has crowned You
King over all!

We, too, would know You,
Though we are small;
We want to love You,
Follow Your call.

How close have you come to giving up?

The first Christmas

happened because of Christ's surrendered will:

"As He was coming into the world, He said: 'You did not want sacrifice and offering, but You prepared a body for Me. . . . Then I said, 'See, I have come . . . to do Your will, O God!'" (Hebrews 10:5,7).

Calvary

happened because of Christ's surrendered will:

"He fell on His face, praying, 'My Father! If it is possible, let this cup pass from Me. Yet not as I will, but as You will'" (Matthew 26:39).

All God's magnificent purposes

—for your own life and for the entire flow of eternal history—

happen because of surrendered wills:

"Therefore, brothers, by the mercies of God, I urge you to present your

bodies as a living sacrifice, holy and pleasing to God . . . so that you may

discern what is the good, pleasing, and perfect will of God" (Romans 12:1,2).

How far can you trust an invisible God?

The virgin Mary—just a young girl—had a bold faith in a great God! What else could explain her total surrender to Him? When told she was going to give birth to the Son of God, her response was, *"Consider me the Lord's slave. . . . May it be done to me according to your word"* (Luke 1:38).

We might say, "Mary! What about Joseph? What's he going to think? And what will he do to you?" But Mary seems to say, "That's God's business. I rest in His ability to take care of me."

"What about the townspeople? What about the rumors?"

Calmly, evenly: "I trust the Lord about them, too."

Did Mary lose? No way. She is still honored and loved the world over. Friend, when you surrender to God's plan for your life, you never lose. That's not risky. In the long run, in fact, it's the only safe thing to do.

Surrender is foundational to life. The world says that surrender is not fair, that it's undemocratic. You might not get your rights, they say. You have to stay in control of your own life!

Oh, we promise you, that's the road to misery and failure. God loves you just as He loved Mary, and He will only do you good. Humble yourself, then, and tell Him (as she told the angel) *"May it be done to me according to your word."*

All over the world, when people humble themselves and surrender to God, they find a freedom and a future unlike any they could have manufactured through their own self-will.

Do yourself a big favor; you do the same.

What awesome news! In ancient stall
A Babe was born—too weak, too small
For most around to comprehend
How far His power would extend.

He is the Mighty God!

Give Him your praise,
Your frankincense and myrrh,
Your bended knee.
Give Him the joys and tears of all your days,
Your life,
Your soul,
Your strength,
Your piety.

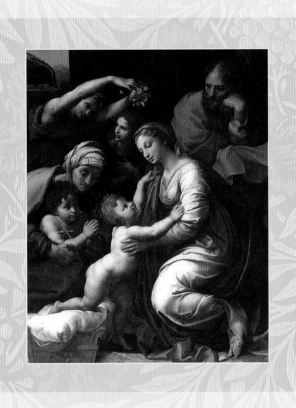

Here come people stealing, stealing
To the Christmas manger stall.
Oh, what wonder they are feeling—
Awe and wonder now revealing—
Hushed before the crib so small!

Those who come, come meekly,
weakly,
Those who come, come dumbly,
humbly,
Or they cannot come
at all.

Who is this baby—meek and mild?
Who is this humble Christmas child?

Humbling becomes us sinners. When God's Spirit is deeply at work in us, we humble ourselves (hard as it is to swallow our pride) and pray and seek His face and turn from our wicked ways—and God hears, forgives, and heals (2 Chronicles 7:14).

But why should Almighty God humble Himself? Here is the mystery of Christmas.

"Out of the ivory palaces

Into a world of woe;

Only His great, eternal love

Made my Savior go."

Christ had always, eternally, been alive and active. *"In the beginning was the Word,"* says John 1:1 — and that reaches back before Genesis 1:1, before creation! Writes Frederick Bruehner,

> *"Just as His death was not the end of Him,*
> *So His birth was not the beginning of Him."*

He was Almighty God.

And yet He came into this world that first Christmas and *"emptied Himself by assuming the form of a slave, taking on the likeness of men"* (Philippians 2:7). Incredible! He created everything — and then He voluntarily submitted to His own creation.

Truly, profoundly, Christ Jesus humbled Himself.

O Christmas Child—
The Son of God, the Savior,
O tiny Babe—
Creation's Joy and Crown,
O Holy One—
The LORD of all forever:

We come before Your mercy seat,
Where wise men of the ages meet.
We lay our treasures at Your feet
And
bow
down.

Part Five

Immanuel
Will Be with You

And remember,

I am with you always, to the end of the age.

Matthew 28:20

Could you boldly face the future if you knew God was with you?

"Now all this took place to fulfill what was spoken by the Lord through the prophet: 'See, the virgin will be with child and give birth to a son, and they will name Him Immanuel,' which is translated 'God is with us'" (Matthew 1:22–23).

"Immanuel." Let's take the name apart. The end "-el" is a name for God: "The Strong One." You see it in:

"Beth-el" (House of God),

"Ishma-el" (God will hear),

"Dani-el" (God the Judge), and so on.

And "Immanuel" means, "God, the Strong One, is with us."

"Immanuel" — "God with us"

But He's not "with us" to spy on us, to "get the scoop" on us, or condemn us. The Apostle Paul wrote that the Lord who is with us is also for us! Listen to Romans 8:31–32: *"If God is for us, who is against us? He did not even spare His own Son, but offered Him up for us all; how will He not also with Him grant us everything?"*

He came to us at Christmas and died for us at Calvary that He might be "with us"—here, now, and forever.

And when you believe that and receive Him, from then on He refuses to be without you, ever again.

A while back some missionaries were imprisoned in China, and they weren't allowed even to talk to each other. With time they grew hungry, cold, and discouraged. One had figured out a calendar system for keeping track of the days, and eventually he knew it was Christmas Day.

He fashioned letters from straw on the floor, and—without the guards noticing—put together the word "IMMANUEL."

When the light of understanding dawned on the other prisoners' faces, suddenly it seemed as if that miserable cell began to glow with Christmas light. The light was the truth of God's real presence with them . . . at that very moment . . . in their cell. Christ was there! He knew what they were experiencing. He understood, and He would help.

"Immanuel"

This Christmas season, write yourself a card with the word *"Immanuel"* on it.

When you get up in the morning, read it: *Immanuel!*

When you face trouble of any kind, read it: *Immanuel!*

When you walk alone, when you talk on the phone, when you meet a friend, when you go to work or church or home, read your reminder: *Immanuel!*

The truth of that name will keep you steady and strong and happy, not just at Christmas, but throughout the coming year. God is with you, and *"in His presence is fullness of joy"!*

...and they will name Him Immanuel, which is translated, "God is with us."

Matthew 1:23

Celebrate with us
"Immanuel" —

God in Christ come down on earth to dwell.

Hold within your heart

His awesome nearness;

Celebrate the Holy Presence' dearness.

Christmas joy for us can last all year:

He is here, good friend!

He's really here!

Have you ever been where God is not?

"GOD with us." What a great name—an accurate name—for the Lord Jesus: "GOD."

This truth of God's being with us wasn't new that first Christmas; God had been with people in the past. He'd told Israel, for instance, that in the tabernacle or temple He would meet with them.

But when Jesus came, God reversed it from "Come meet Me in a certain place" to "I am now come to meet you. I've made the first move. I am 'Immanuel.'"

He went from eternity to time. He went from all of heaven to earth, to be literally "with us." Jesus is God, come to join us; He is God settled down among us.

The Gospel of Matthew begins with it: *"They will name Him Immanuel . . . 'God is with us.'"* And later, Matthew ends with Jesus' saying, *"And remember, I am with you always, to the end of the age."*

You cannot be where God is not.

"With" in the King James Version of the Bible is not only a preposition; it's also a noun. In Judges 16:7, Samson declared that his strength would leave him if he were tied with seven "withs." It was a word for vines so fresh and strong that they were virtually impossible to break. When two things were tied with "withs," they were together for good!

"And 'round my heart still closely twined
Those cords which naught can sever;
For I am His and He is mine
Forever and forever!"

Friend, think about it; hug it to your heart:

    In times of threatened health, *Immanuel!*

        In times of financial crunch, *Immanuel!*

    In times of spiritual doubt, *Immanuel!*

        In times of job problems, *Immanuel!*

    In times of bereavement, *Immanuel!*

        In times of difficulties, *Immanuel!*

As you right now think on this, *Immanuel!*

Through all your Christmas season and beyond, *Immanuel!*

You're safe.
God is with you.

He has been with you.
He is with you now.
And He will be with you…
Always.

Why settle for "God with me" when you can have "God with us"?

Jesus moved steadily, determinedly, from heaven to the manger, to the cross, to the resurrection, and then to His Church—His own ones. We're an occupied people! And we take our place as His people with all who have loved and followed Him for two thousand years—as well as with all those who follow Him today.

He is God with us, together. We are at our best when we treat each other with care and love, because Christ is with each one of us, and yet also, with all of us. He is Immanuel!

Moses insisted on the literal presence of the Lord as he led God's people forward together toward the Promised Land. He said, *"If your Presence does not go with us, do not send us up from here. How will anyone know that you are pleased with me and with your people unless* you go with us? What else will distinguish me and your people from all the other people on the face of the earth?"* (Exodus 33:15–16, NIV).

And the God of grace and glory said to Moses, *"My Presence will go with you, and I will give you rest"* (Exodus 33:14, NIV).

Oh, insist on the presence of Immanuel for your whole family, for your whole church! If the circle is incomplete right now, or at odds with each other, intercede for them passionately, as Moses did! Ask the Lord, *"How will anyone know that You are pleased with me, with us —?"* Ask Him, *"What else will distinguish us from all the other people of the earth —?"*

Lead the way in apologies to your family, your church; be humble; be broken; take the low road. And behind the scenes . . . pray and pray and pray.

"Immanuel" means "God with us —together!"

"The LORD is in His Holy House."
Oh, grace beyond describing,
That Christ should please to dwell in me,
Immanuel residing!
"My soul doth magnify the Lord,"
I sing with little Mary,
That God should choose to enter in
This humble sanctuary!

Not now in little Bethlehem,
As in the tender story;
Not now upon the mercy seat,
The bright Shekinah glory,
But in the body of His saint
He now makes His residing —
Both He in me and I in Him,
In fellowship abiding.

Within my heart, a burning bush;
Within, a mountain smoking;
This flesh of mine, a temple veil,
The wondrous Presence cloaking;
Within this broken earthenware
A high and holy treasure:
Oh, mystery of mysteries!
Oh, grace beyond all measure!

"The LORD is in His Holy House."
Mysterious habitation!
I feel His Presence here within
And offer my oblation.
Keep burning, incense of my soul!
Keep cleansing me, O laver!
I want to serve and praise my God
Forever and forever!

Family Reflections

Last July the family was at daughter Margie and John's house, celebrating Ray's birthday. (Ray says, "Patriarch, with the accent on the first syllable—pay!")

What a mob! Daughter Sherry and Walt were there with two of their three: Mindy, youth worker on the staff of their church, and Beth Anne at Biola University. Drew was ministering in Mongolia with other teenagers for the summer.

Margie and John's offspring were there: Lisa and husband Mark with their toddlers, William and Wesley; Laurie and husband Mike with their little Kaitlin and Patrick; John IV and bride Becky.

Ray, Jr., had flown in for the party from Augusta, leaving behind wife Jani, as well as children Eric (student at Trinity Evangelical Divinity School), Krista and Dane (both at Wheaton College), and high schooler Gavin.

Nels and Heather were there with little sons Bradford and Robbie.

We ate a glorious meal with the volume level at the ceiling. Eventually the two little grandsons and the four great grandchildren disappeared off to bed. Whew!

The remaining seventeen of us gathered in the living room to talk, laugh, share silly cards, and eventually get down to our birthday party ritual: telling what we love about the birthday person and then having group prayer for that one.

It was a tender time—precious, as always. Our birthday parties are times to be guarded carefully (we're all busy people) and times to be cherished. God alone knows how long the circle will be unbroken.

Beautiful things were said to Ray, godly things with deep meanings.

Along the way, Mike (married to granddaughter Laurie) spoke. "I remember the first family birthday party I got invited to. Laurie and I were dating," he said. "Oh, my gosh! My eyes and ears couldn't get enough. So much love! Sins were prayed for, joys got expressed. It was a "God thing." I thought, *The Lord is here. The Lord is within this circle of people. This is awesome! I want into this family!*" (Laughter.)

Then he said very kind things about the Birthday Boy.

Ray ended the prayer time something like this:

"Father, who am I? Who are any of us? We are all at best unprofitable servants. We have nothing good in us, in ourselves. Lord—and that's all right.

"May our family only be explainable by the fact that you are our God! Individually and together, You have saved us, and You are with us! You are our Immanuel!

"Oh, as long as we live may we each choose only to walk with You, by You, for You, in You—obedient to You, drawing from You, dependent on You, loving You.

"Continue to be Immanuel to us, O Lord! As John and Charles Wesley said, *'And best of all, God is with us!'*"

Do not be afraid...

Said God to trembling Jacob, "Do not be afraid;
Go down to Egypt; I will bless you there."
Said God to threatened Israel, "Do not be afraid;
I'll guard you with my tender, loving care."

Said God through Christmas angels, "Do not be afraid;
Your Savior has been born; be full of cheer!
The price for all your trespasses will soon be paid.
Believe how much I love you! Do not fear."

And through the centuries since, and in the days ahead,
He is Almighty God! He'll lead as He has led.
His mercies will endure. His grace will aid.
So Merry Christmas! Do not be afraid.

List of Illustrations:

Cover	The Adoration of the Shepherds, Jean Francois de Troy
p. 7	The Annunciation to the Shepherds, Nicolaes Pietersz Berchem
11	Adoration of the Shepherds, Caravaggio
19	The Visitation, Portormo
25	The Doni Tondo, Michelangelo
26	Adoration of the Shepherds, Agnolo Bronzino
33	The Nativity, Coreggio
40	St. Joseph with the Infant Jesus, Guido Reni
42	The Holy Family, Palma Vecchio
47	Christ and the Samaritan Woman, Bernardo Strozzi
48	The Supper at Emmaus, Titian
57	Head of Christ, Rembrandt
58	Adoration of the Shepherds, Hugo van der Goes
61	Adoration of the Shepherds, Gerrit van Honthorst
71	Nativity with St. Francis, Caravaggio
77	Deposition, Caravaggio
79	The Holy Trinity, El Greco
89	The Adoration of the Magi, Jacopo Bassano
93	Adoration of the Kings, Fray Juan Bautista Maino
94	The Annunciation, Tintoretto
98	The Holy Family, Raffaello Sanzio
102	Adoration of the Magi, Botticelli
105	The Ascension, Benjamin West
111	Simeon, Rembrandt
115	Christ in the House of Martha and Mary, Jan Vermeer van Delft
125	The Transfiguration, Raffaello Sanzio